Partially

Kept

Partially

Kept

Martha Ronk

NIGHTBOAT BOOKS

CALLICOON, NEW YORK

Part One

Partially

Kept

The poems in Part 1 keep certain phrases and vocabulary from Sir Thomas Browne's essay *The Garden of Cyrus* (1658).

Light that makes things seen, makes some things invisible. . . .

Or

Or on a morning

> *the wistful eyes which whilom glanced down upon the fields*

Or on a morning

> *I wot not, what in mee is come to pass, In me this wilom*
> *who most gladly was*

Or on a morning that came after, after the fields

lanceleaf blue or only the fields

where I was distanced from the past and from the time I saw it,

eyes having changed in the meanwhile, who was walking the morning,

the morning moving through blue having never, not that I am or what is in me,

the morning moving gladly, is now come to pass.

By parallaxis

For if one could see out of the dark chamber of just plain going about things

out of the past where many things are known,

as some are seen, that is by Parallaxis,

or at some distance from their true and proper beings—

the wingy divisions

reddish accumulations pooling

the startled recognitions of what was flapping

or hearing the air loosed in the pipes,

then birds mouthing themselves into cardinals, one sister calling

the other to tell what she saw.

Sound

Let me not be, or being   only in the gravel

the brushed sound it makes underfoot

or under that or before the foot hits the ground

in the undoing of stone into gravel, the breaking apart

and then into sand at the shore where I left off.

It was a beautiful day.

The dunes at Sand Mountain in Nevada sing a note of low C.

The Quincunx

```
        O     O
           O
        O     O
```

In muddy waters apt to breed Duckweed, and Periwinkles

a resemblance hereof there is

     and some resemblance there

     is of this order

     neatly declaring

     order in all things

thus hath Nature planted the Leaves in the Head of the common and prickled Artichoak;

the same also found in the pricks, sockets, and impressions of the seeds, in the pulp or bottome

     a like correspondency

     and beforehand

     when the other is also perceptible

breeding an accumulating Artifice.

Things observable

While he saith, with incredible Artifice hath Nature framed

where by the way we cannot but wish we might examine

all things observable by land and sea,

yet with what eyes do I see

with what judgments do I judge

who stumbles about in the multitudes,

calls up darknesses upon darknesses

undoes all knitted into raveled care

mistakes the River Tigris for Euphrates.

My partial tongue

Unknown plants brought from remoter Countries.

A way of uttering.

Once having found it, then saying it outloud in the vicinity of several.

Or putting it down.

After a while we do get somewhere plentiful—

an unnoticed lapse or filament

a sprouting in Glasses of water

the names themselves

(*the Spongy leaves of some Sea-wracks*)

voicing as errant as germination.

Whither has wandered now my partial tongue?

The particular state wherein you reside

Wherein is one formulated as another

as the air thins into finer threads on climbing

and what marks transition at the edge of tree line—

that bird seems larger in this altitude, larger as the air it scopes,

at the base of the blue alpines, falling as a catapult,

the centrifugal force extending into wingspan and beakspan

and dizziness at the pit of the stomach, its insides deeper,

a form of another entirely relegated to if not related to

the particular state wherein you reside.

Grafting

by conjoining plants of very different natures in parts, barks, lateness
and precocities

      piecemeal, an oak perchance
its branch-like exposure

the expostulation of
its gnarled shrugs, its overhangingness

the close application of shadows
and a closer cool internal to them

or speech and the modulations thereof
various in the variously given

and assumptions out of which formations and other plant-like

extrusions   all sorts of experiments

though the considerable rules, the elocutions, fructifications

      the cut

the ususual and practised course of insitions

a time-erased touch   letters tactically revised

the stalks of mint

the stalks of mint set in glasses with the root end upward & out of the water

sending forth sprouts without the aid of roots

or a thought, reasonable enough, but not even a thought

      of a face never to be seen again

a configuration drawn with thin ink,   a face and she had seen it too,

the root stripped from the leaves

      knowing this all this afternoon, nothing to do with leaves

      yet to touch them, to lift the mint into the air,

      as if the configuration of it

would hold what's sketched in—

      a nervous line, her.

Alpines

For the length of time it took, taking us then

all unmindful until the later part of the morning

pushing up through the narrows above the snow line

then the distance divideth into the ascending and descending portion

as germination being the push

through the narrow Navell and hole about the midst of the stone

yet the unearthly silence was what would interrupt and overtake us

indomitable   as pushing through stone.

The fold

flowers are pentagonally wrappen up

A fold in the lip of a petal

    and yellow and bending over to get it

to whom it may be addressed,

to whom the *give me* and *take me* and listening as if I were listening in

    as closely as never I can

stooped and tying up a shoe

what would it sound like if we were folded in on

if everyone were away

    bending over in the grass to get the small ones

    listening to echoes and duplications and then

to sit there, hunched over, waiting.

Restless

                              early summer shaking as aspens

observable in the closing of the eyes, closing and opening

where so much is, between, behind,

what I see, what I can't and haven't the names for

                              pendulous excrescencies of severall Trees, of Wallnuts,

        Alders, and Hazels,

        for the circles in Trees are naturally concentricall, parallell unto the bark,

and unto

        each other

glimpsed in time-lapse, seeing into and close up, sight unraveling at this distance

as vision and visionary spin their concentric circles around the trees

MARTHA RONK

and yet, could we ever satisfy ourselves, restless

as the blown rain.

Refusal

Thus hath nature ranged the flowers

                    that the richest

odour of plants surpasseth and astonisheth

                  yet doth not

suffice.

Downpour

Come at me without motive parts now that I think of it,

but what I was thinking, angular, drenching,

but inquiring into it in any case, a monologue perhaps,

for my ears alone, speaking and again speaking,

not to my ears, music to mine own, permitting not so many to speak,

the one guided by the ten-stringed harp of the shepherd

      even the speaker of her own speaking in her own ear

      the figure coming, drenching the fields.

The bittern

The cellist died in the morning paper under another tent,

front door open for what air there is, for air

      hiding behind it, the obit, *the birds most multiplied,*

the bird hidden in a book read once

the newspaper mercurial

      a secretive bird

      the sounds of the morning resumed

      its far-carrying cry.

Incision

The networks and nets of antiquity

shall we prie into it

unearthing the difficult past onto the blank page

all is foreign in this mental state we find ourselves in, yet

the rose at first is thought to have been of five leaves as it

yet groweth wilde among us

despair upon incision

become a point of art.

Drowning

Plants on the surface of the water

wild lilies without root and stem

pale fabric snatched from the undertow

                                          those melodious lays

floating   above her muddy death

and the awkward bundle of blouses and skirts

the balloons of gabardine on the surface

water itself unable to maintain its stony silence.

Indistinguishable

that white flowers have yellow thrums

that true seeds are indistinguishable by old eyes

lost as if in a blur and lying in perpetual shades

      either under the leaf or in coverings

the beginning of each phrase drops away unheard

meaningless even if repeated

what can't be seen and what once was yellow

alyssum in the distance

unravels perforce,

      and shades scatter between.

Position

And if the pot were turned the leaves

would work themselves into their former declinations,

leaving by leaving,

turn and precisely tell us

as who wouldn't in a matter of days

find oneself elsewhere,

moving east to get west

finding a former inclination

the obtuse but seldom found, what question was it to which

only position answered.

Manifest

Underneath, beyond the stand of trees, the oak

manifesting upon incision the signature of a Starre.

Signs lodged below the surface, or

                into the past, garbled, hushed—

walk into the kitchen, say something to keep the overhead bulb an overhead bulb

try to remember the woman there

underneath the years, underneath the tree,

                let her walk up the steps, into the room.

Colour

Alterable, answerable unto an adjustment to the surroundings

which first altereth into this colour

purple unto blue, blue unto green

all the possibilities hanging in, in the slightest sway

in the ever-changing complexion of the sky,

the turn of phrase, the way it softens when you say something,

as the color of a vowel sound, a new shade of meaning

having sat at the table set out in the air,

the green metal chairs, the peeling paint

the scraping sound moved about and the lowering of the sky.

Tendrils

whereon they hang

        Thyme, Savory

either side-spreading or tap roots, it matters not

        the tendrils of the Clementine

or a segue into the bottom and shady recesses of the sea

        coral caverns intricate as plant systems underground and lit from above

        where one moves effortlessly through unimagined territories

                with ease, aplomb,

ceasing to breathe.

Simple

The unsparing spare,

the line in Turgenev's suicide note,

"I could not simplify myself."

Reaching a point that's never reached, the doorways.

Up there in the potager you could see it was held by raveling twine, yet it
        kept them out and in.

But the old sepulchral bed in the market-place of Megara
        was in the form of a Lozenge; readily made out by the composure of the body.

The door itself opening, the body in the form of, passing through,

framed by it and can one think of reaching out and not touching it

is that what it would be like

      air at the fingertips, oneself in the strict form of a lozenge

      if I could simplify myself.

      It floats there like the garden at the top of the hill,

                            that "if."

The

When having finished   the

              the beginning again, the article

in the root of Water fern, every eye may discern the form of a Half Moon

everyone, every eye, every age disappears

                    a dissolving moon, nothing to be seen through the smoke and ashes

the sentence itself an integument of flexible green, evoking

beginning and end

a half mirrored   a whole   a half and beginning again—

and discernment, the quiet of parsing

the streets stilled

ruins one's ancestors recall and filmic versions of the same

the   root of a water fern and time enough   for the

Part Two

No

Sky

Relics

In this month the tea is cold before you get to it and the rhododendron all leaves
for another year and she says Buddhists revere relics as well and worship teeth and
bones from the ashes and she's finished a whole set of revisions and will keep after
it and I hear on the morning news a cashier in France has written a book saying
mothers in line threaten their whiny children with growing up to be cashiers and
the reliquaries hold bones in silver as elaborate as the pistils of jack-in-the-pulpits
as sparrows eat the coats of oil off the radiators of cars as daylilies collapse in time-
lapse, as the farmer hefts a bag of grain on his shoulders going up the hill never
thinking anything about it past the white llama, the famous Himalayan flower,
meth labs and twenty-five days of rain in mid summer, a left-over stripe of silver
across the sky.

Needful

Needful's is a word to look up, to dismiss, almost all this, this August
still needing to say something, seeing it looming, is it too soon, too late,
her voice unfounded, yet where were you in the aftermath, I ask myself
needing some sort of answer for the pronoun herself for after all how's one
to proceed into the month that comes after, voicing to the shadowy remnants
along the expanse of lawn into streams out of which all mythology was destined
to occur sooner or later, spilling forth sylphs and syllables of assurance
without knowing whose experience is having whom or to whom
in the green and hazy hedge of summer it is incumbent to speak.

A slight thing

Impingement as slight pressure
as slight as her glance, distracted,
from where as a slice of light in and out of the slats
the consequence measured but the source traced back,
waning. The window hard,
the light impermanent and unquestionably deft.
A slight thing transparent as wings trapped against the glass,
shifting as the intermittent light,
lost in its own pledge to it.

A preconceived idea

Within the angle of light should always be a tree out the window
an evocation of black and white, the happenstance of arrangement
anonymity making a clearing, a twist of segments drawn on a backdrop

a reconnoitering until it's all over and everyone calls it a day,
takes off down steps or steps off the platform and then in frenzy of wind,
in the confusions of all that comes up when different minds consort

one can often hear the objection that it is all unconvincingly tree-like
from the perspective of the figure who's seen it from a second story window
activating the leaves more or less as suits the restless torso

but alternately muted, a formal note of moderate length
and where to begin but in the oblong leaves, the bend of the willow
the one with the absence of all but an angled tendency

a sense of fading into the distance, the strokes feathering off at the end
everything in attendance in the atmosphere's exchange of air and tree
as novel in its entirety as any preconceived idea.

West wind

A window in the remainder of the third chapter brings forth a warm storm of lightning,
curling the covers of books, typing even faster, a hypocritical attitude of spine and fervor
propels you past interrogating the text and eating everything and fending distraction
and it's obvious that authors employ windows as if escaping into gardens (real
or otherwise) and without directly offering the interlocutor a satisfying answer
or taking up direct address even to the elements which in another era
would have satisfied and stimulated endeavor (although I point to the lack of wind
even from the west), but this rain straight down and hard puts you more directly
in the material world one hates to lose given possibilities latent therein.

Aporia

One certainty replaced by yet another certainty,
creating in the aporia the flutter and disconcertion of indecision
and the simultaneous recognition of the consequences
for one's habitual maneuvers and the labyrinthine pathways
profoundly nebulous and lacking constellate formations,
as if loopy attention could be described only as perfunctory haunt,
a hollowed-out arena of wandering and a better grasp of the Gothic,
the confluence of *the man in the crowd* and a meager life,
perorations of dissolution determinate of syntax and tone,
plus impassable and paltry notions of sublimity.

A photograph of a side window

How close it seems, dusty leaves patterning the siding with shadows,
open half-way for air on what must be a summer night,
an eternal return located in its technological reproducibility,
its time repeating, its grasses and the feeling of grass, never simply itself,
but moving forward as walking across it to get to the window
and the rarity of seeing oneself in the glass reflection by chance
and wondering how she got out of the place she's usually in,
the past most frequently, but occasionally a future not too distant
given the common fear of the photograph propped on the bureau
where she and the others served cups from the momentous tablecloth
spread corner to corner at a 40 degree angle to the side of the house
as the day faded in the original of which this is only a copy
calling up what never was in the tonal variations of gray
as the house is only a material copy of *house* writ large, exposed
as the flesh and bone, coats and jackets of the lived again.

Reading & Writing & Stealing

I'm suddenly afraid that in the end I have stolen something—

the large bird, the large flakes of blackened paper quivering in the grate

information pulled from the surroundings as from a fire,

fingers burning, a manuscript saved from some film I saw last night.

She holds the phone to the air so I can hear the geese flying overhead,

their bodies improbably lifted, their cries staticy on this end.

Each item put next to the other so something will be yielded up,

some analogy squeezed from the proximity or from the way

she stands in the field by the farmhouse at an angle to the fence looking up.

I never see what she sees in what sounds like crying.

The wind quickens the fire and as she moves closer

I try to catch the headlines before they're swallowed up.

After visiting for a time it is time to go (with umbrella)

After several days it feels normal every day and then the approach of leaving

takes it away and what's passing coalesces into things out of place

    standing there in the middle unable to catch hold

a poppy split in two   a conversation veering away

the corroded structure in the distance coming down piece by piece

particles rearranging around us in the leaving of it

at the end of his life Emerson kept forgetting the names of things, *the thing that people*
    take away with them

description itself might be called a place from which to leave

a detailing of what will become metaphors configured vine and branch-like
(boxwood, clematis, shapes of lichen mapping out a stone)

forms of intent out of place when we aren't where we were.

No sky

after Robert Adams *California Views*

No sky   a gray backdrop merely and absence
and below: the scraggle of dusty fronds, the scrub oak and scrub jay
whose abrasive noises sharpen in response.

Shadows proliferate in deep furrows   no sky above
merely a scrim registering conical thrusts, a heightened flurry &
outlines of branches, the dead ones slowly petering out.

magnificent ruin   the cut through the field   blasted chaparral

As I understand my job, it is, while suggesting order, to make things appear as much as possible
to be the way they are in normal vision.

An unvoiced series of sentences, without articulation,
with gray shapes, formulating a syntax loosening and then tightening from edge to edge.

The frame sets a border from which a thin straggle hangs down at random &
like purposeful intrusion, and so unlike

and the interstate (in the title) missing from the photograph itself
merely a dry riverbed, the density of shadows trapped in the confusion
of bush and bush-like tree

except from higher up than the rest, its thin trunk arched against

                                                        no sky

colorless, less often remarked upon, appositely emotionless these days,
a relic, like the fan palm living at the edges of water.

Elegy

Headlights light up a weed or cone of blossoms lifting off into shadows
driven by the demarcation of time.
They are forever back there as we go forward in the undifferentiated dark.

Part of the trouble is the echo of objects just past and to a lesser degree,
those about to arrive.

                                                       They fade out slowly
those conical bright shapes out from the field & across the dashboard.

He had walked into/ fallen into the truck crossing the road.
Later he had fallen into the water near the pier.
Earlier he had decided or he hadn't decided or it had shaped itself around him.

It's hard to see the sunflowers in the dark but the dark center surrounded
by the many gray petals is immediately clear, despite shadows,
despite tricks played on the eye.

It seems more than obvious that nothing particular is about to happen.

When the painters paint the white line down the middle of the road do they see
how it shines in the near dark nearly upon us.

Reading her thinking

What is it to read someone's thinking or to watch a thought as this morning for no reason

    driving in the car with her I could, despite difficulty, follow a silent corridor,

    a grassy cut through the field, the excellence of coherence, a divergent, occasional

view

Nor could I, caught up as it is possible to be, cut myself off from the ways in which she

    meandered from one possibility to another as if it were a normal thing,

    an everyday thing that everyone takes part in, albeit unbeknownst and often

denied

Like fitting the doors into swollen frames, gauging the week to come, assuring

    one another after preconceptions set aside, inquiries made, halted only

    by chance as when the weather shifts, clouds part and alignment is necessarily

interrupted

Yet hesitations can go on endlessly while waiting for the moment to return,

    in which hearing another's thoughts is as palpable as ozone before the storm

and one can shuffle responses to a variety of shifts so unlike the spoken word
word

So that even when I write to her it is no longer necessary to lay out the various enigmas

of the place changing year by year, since all the unknowables and mysteries,

all hapless additions—far ahead of the regular mail—will have already
arrived

Incomplete form

The African basket hangs from the rafters who ever thought to use the word *rafter*

    yet the weaving of emptiness made for collections and storage, a flamboyant

    leap forward as the hollowing out forecasts harvests and tomorrow's
crop

After one's decided how the days will play out it is nonetheless impossible not to

    rearrange the order of events, the insatiable habits of mind that put one in front of

    the other and play it backward as if we were all trained with film and reels on our
minds

These practices unlike the threading of reeds or forming of what is needful, but rather

    a useless and time-consuming practice often leading to difficulties unpredictable

    often ruinous to others concerned as in *I've decided otherwise and will come after*
all

How much we want to disobey the ways things are set to go or have gone before, as if

    it were built into the DNA we carry about with us unlike the quenching of thirst unlike the collecting of reeds, a needless invention of how it might have gone otherwise

Such that it is no longer hanging there, I never made that statement, rerun backwards

takes the story to an extension far better than the so-called end-point itself

and we conclude that our minds must govern despite the consequences, ultimate remorse

.

Interpretation

A blue under her tired eyes, the repository of memory without recourse to revision

      beneficial practices or the even-handed and matter-of-fact—simply the mark

      as a watermark once on paper or the interpretation written in long-hand at
intervals

The interpreter of the text laid the book aside and the warnings against over-reading

      stood out in the lengthy paragraphs and the delicacy of her skin underscored

      the slight discoloration that was inherited from her grandmother on her mother's
side

Still for many days the rain continued to fall and the sentences were read aloud and

      the difficulty of maintaining neutrality increased as the margins revealed hand-

      written commentary she'd made years before although her memory of it had
lapsed

Along with the phosphorescence on the ground on the very night or the show of shooting

      stars from the rooftop or a random confusion passed to her by someone else,

all of it marginal to an existence taken up by innovations minimal and highly discrete

yet ever subject to change as were the books now almost ruined by constant rain

and convoluted habits taken up in the company of like-minded souls known

only for a time at that particular time of a life, scattered now as abandoned fascicles

Events

Allowances had to be made given the circumstances and voices carried in the thin air

      taken apart limb by limb and clearing the deck for what might be spoken

      as one waits for the echo and the valley itself, as waiting becomes part of
it

Nothing can be separated out, and yet deciding what belongs prolongs the discussion

      as something one returns to thinking through after the event itself

      if events can be said to end or to have a clear beginning for which one needs
craft

The waiting takes more time than measured by any instrument or separation into acts

      made up of discrete moments and the relationship between gestures or furnishings

      arranged at another time but adding randomly to what is expected to
arrive

At the time it seemed it would never end yet after it did the earlier and impatient analysis

      seemed unrelated to the thing itself and the difficulties of moving so many

across the lawn when previously what was to happened seemed conceptually
clear

But events themselves are circumscribed by participatory and willing obsession,

an unspoken agreement to allow oneself to be encircled by whatever ensues

neglecting what came before and what is to come for the purpose of perfecting
form

An exceptional reality

It was now much darker, although the little daylight left had an exceptional reality as if it were outside me. I thought that someone was standing on the other side and went to join her in a space that resembled a space more thoroughly familiar than one would have thought. I had an idea to assign her a task that would have required persistence, but then there was the usual delay and a scarcely perceptible shift of light as if whatever had been conceived now had to be abandoned. Increasingly the space began to thin into the emptiness reflected back at me as from a mirror viewed from an angle in which one's profile is missing.

I couldn't be mistaken about this calm: it was like a place I'd seen before which was, however, not located here or in the immediate environs so far as I could determine, but rather at a remove and yet a remove that seemed both distanced and near at hand as if one could reach out and touch the pocket of warm water that hides itself in a cold sea, remarkable for its limits and its saturation.

Diffusion was a necessary component of the reality as much as its vividness, a diffusion like a thin tone into which one leans to hear, attending with care to that which one can scarcely make out, that draws one, tilts one's body in the direction of and brings about the union of oneself and that other thing that without the diffusion and blur would remain colorless and indistinct, but with it allows the sails to fill with wind, the halyard to snap hard against the mast.

What does not take place must occur over and over again as one continues to wait for it and if one wants it deeply enough one must actually work to prevent its happening lest by its happening it be reduced and delimited. One's entire effort must go towards keeping it from happening so that it can loop in one's memory without cessation; and yet this effort is itself so demanding that all becomes mere persistence.

Part Three

August

Remembrance

You have to write what you don't yet know and hope

that in another time you might.

But there will be no French

even if he translates some few words to help.

He's ordered more birds to replace those lost

and the few scatter, leaving bits of white.

No one can free himself from the manner of his time

and even he didn't believe he was invited where he received invitations to go.

The yellow bird was up the road and took off quickly

though not so quickly as the swallows skimming the field at the end of the day—

I couldn't believe there were so many and couldn't see what they were after.

Underneath the crescendo the sounds of footsteps

although he'd gone up hours ago.

Even in another tongue, it's something like the thing itself.

Re-reading

Then one could see where it had been all along.

Then on puts a hand over a mouth.

One never gets over that the plant repeats itself growing out of itself

and there it is again on the top of a hill.

I've gotten so that I avoid passing by but this week there are so many others

and one comes to understand pilgrimage as walking.

I was thinking of it only yesterday how we have lost the road,

the sounds on the pavement severing other sounds—

the turkeys wild in the un-cut fields,

the line of them scattering their wings.

This part of a life must be producing a decided next part.

August

The Nicotiana is a paler green,

not only behind a hedge, not only in the dark.

You can hear it with your eyes closed.

It's louder than reaching anyone else, talking,

for example, to the piano lessons one was given.

It was percussive, seemed to linger unimportantly all morning.

There wasn't supposed to be any today

but light manages to turn it around,

the periphery sneaking in

in its high-pitched and convincing way.

Then August comes that very day, and so do we, finally,

step across the threshold, bang a hip into the swollen door,

wait for the impatient wind to burn itself out.

The ardor

All the slim importance on the surface of her dress

her hair and the tinny thing as well.

Nothing rhapsodizes so easily as the here and now.

Who said what I am said to have said,

red berries in an expanse of well-watered green.

The future's invasive, a stolen sentence or two.

A deep sound and my own blue sky.

It's a miracle of a day if you've been elsewhere

but I could never take that photograph seriously

with angles going this way and that,

a garden built in the midst of power-lines

and no place to stand and then too it could have been the ardor

even when I remember only the intervening portent.

MARTHA RONK

Let Rhetoric

Echoes of the future, not yet

rather a bit of mauve, the color flat,

out on a thin stem.

Any echo will do,

let rhetoric take over the silence foretelling billions of years,

let color.

Not that red, but geranium red in the sun

over the phone explaining.

I walk out and under the bush with the red berries

branches needing to be pruned.

The work of the mind is endless as the word for how many years it's been

since the world began. *How many years it's been*, I say,

walk out and look for a color I've never seen.

Dangling modifier

The poem a cylinder   enclosing silence

a dangling modifier, as in "when having entered, a coat,"

the slippery pleasure of her shoulders revealed,

winter, the halls cold and dangerous,

Anne exposed   and more.

Orlando

Having arrived,

                        there in the foot just off the ground

observing one's own ankle just there   out in front.

Now August,   the orange cosmos not having yet arrived,

they float on a long stem from the distance of old eyes,

multitudes tempting as moons

the ankle a stab of desire, a drowning in the sea

having arrived at these stony places, numerous tricks of sight

all things blurred by night   she not thinking she would ever be

unable to imagine the weather on this coast.

With color

When having entered,   a yellow bush

that time of year without and within

all one wants is the repetition of it, not so much to ask

not so much   the fact of it not hard to pull off,

it comes without anything one could do and what it does is deep within—with
color,

forsythia sprigs of one sort

or another   deep collapse into a side yard, only this,

          when having entered a side yard

that other spring.

A sickly Polaroid

Remembering the acts of oblivion,

working to forget a damp afternoon

one's arm on the wooden chair

legs in a right angle, the material archive against which our memories rest

ardent postures, guises, ruses

one's arm on the green wooden chair, one's obliviousness to all around

insects erasing all but themselves.

The photograph was a sickly Polaroid, green and washed-out

I forget who else was there.

The remorseless quiet when he says I'm going.

The Polaroid in its sickly green, the Polaroid in one's hand,

the sides of the paper pushed against the sides of the hand,

something damp.

Attachments

Being attached to things outside   the whatever it is

I ask the name of, purple, leggy, right out there

ask someone   for the whatever it is

take it up, pick it off the road, remember its Latin name,

see it on the wall there, black and white,   stalk-like

remember the trees that used to thrive, remember the heatwave

the ones at risk, the vulnerable,

and the accents, remember the accents.

She was in a winter coat, she'd forgotten

the heat

in the heat the flowers   being attached

the wilt.

The light on the water

The lamplight dimming at the end of a hand,

the light dimming the transparent hand,

the eventual fade from view.

The field calm and flat and the first to go as the sky claims all.

It's never as if wind just pushed us along

where there wasn't much and the river was narrow,

the shore seemingly close at hand,

and often we sat for a long time waiting.

It was long ago and I admire now the afternoon,

the outing that had been planned,

the light on the water that might have come.

Notes

Part 1

All the words in italics are taken from Sir Thomas Browne, *The Gardens of Cyrus*; although those of us in the 21st century may share his love of the plant kingdom, we are skeptical of Browne's assurance that nature is divinely and intricately ordered. The poems in *Partially Kept* articulate the frequent illegibility of that past. *In memory of Wayne Winterrowd (1942-2010), plantsman & author.*

"The surface": the incident of drowning dresses is from *The Master*, Colm Toibin. "By parallaxis" is for my sisters; "Manifest" in memory of my mother.

Part 2

"Aporia" references the Edgar Allan Poe story.

Part 3

"Remembrance" evokes *Remembrances of Things Past*.

"Echoes" Let Rhetoric take over": thanks to George Puttenham: *As figures be the instruments of ornament in euer language, so be they also in sorte abuses or rather trespasses in speech, because they passe the ordinary limits of common vtterance, and be occupied of a purpose to deceiue the ear and also the minde. Arte of English Poesie* (1589).

"Dangling modifier" refers to Anne Boleyn.

Acknowledgements

I would like to thank The MacDowell Colony and The National Endowment for the Arts for time to work on this manuscript. Thanks to the following journals in which some of these poems were printed in earlier versions.

"The particular state wherein you reside," Stalks of mint," "Or," "The Bittern": *Colorado Review* 33.1, spring 2006.

"The field," "Above and below ground," "A downpour," "Gazing into the distance": *Carnet de route* 09. 2006. "A downpour": reprinted in the anthology, *Not For Mothers Only*, ed. Catherine Wagner and Rebecca Wolff, Fence Books, 2007.

"Simple," "Manifest," "The," "Colour," "Remembrance," "The Ardor": *The Denver Quarterly* 41.4, 2007.

"Sound": *jubilat* 14, 2007, reproduced as a broadside by Bonfire Press.

"Resemblance," "Position": *Octopus #10*.

"Not only in the dark": *Electronic Poetry Project #8*.

"Incision": *Gulf Coast,* 21.2, summer/fall 2008.

"Alpine," "By Parallaxis," "Dangling Modifier": *Lana Turner*, ed. Calvin Bedient and David Lau, #1 Fall 2008.

"Re-reading": POOL on-line #8 2009.

"Aporia": OR issue #2 April 2009.

"Incomplete Form," "Interpretation": *Denver Quarterly*, #44.2, 2010.

"Tendrils," "The west wind," "Relics": *Interim vol.#20* fall 2011.

"Elegy," "No Sky": *Boston Review*, forthcoming.

"A Photograph of Shadows": *Chicago Review*, forthcoming.

But the Quincunx of Heaven runs low, and 'tis time to close the five ports of knowledge.

ISBN: 978-1-937658-01-4

Design and typesetting by HR Hegnauer
Text set in Meridien
Cover art: photograph from "Weed Series, 1951, Aspen, Colorado" by Ferenc Berko.
Reproduced with permission of the Ferenc Berko Archive.
The author also thanks Steven and Mus White.

Cataloging-in-publication data is available
From the Library of Congress

Distributed by University Press of New England
One Court Street
Lebanon, NH 03766
www.upne.com

Nightboat Books
Callicoon, New York
www.nightboat.org

About Martha Ronk

Martha Ronk is the author of eight previous books of poetry, including *Vertigo*, selected by C.D. Wright for the National Poetry Series, *In a landscape of having to repeat*, recipient of the 2005 PEN USA Award in Poetry, and *Why/Why Not*. She has also published a fictional memoir, *Displeasures of the Table*, and a collection of fiction, *Glass Grapes and Other Stories*. Her poetry is included in the anthologies *Lyric Postmodernisms, American Hybrid,* and *Not For Mothers Only*. She has had residencies at Djerassi and The MacDowell Colony, and taught in the summer programs at the University of Colorado and Naropa. Awarded a 2007 NEA Literature fellowship, she worked as an editor for Littoral Books and *The New Review of Literature*. She is the Irma and Jay Price Professor of English at Occidental College in Los Angeles.

Nightboat Books

Nightboat Books, a nonprofit organization, seeks to develop audiences for writers whose work resists convention and transcends boundaries. We publish books rich with poignancy, intelligence, and risk. Please visit our website, www.nightboat.org, to learn about our titles and how you can support our future publications.

This book was made possible by a grant from the Topanga Fund, which is dedicated to promoting the arts and literature of California.

The following individuals have supported the publication of this book. We thank them for their generosity and commitment to the mission of Nightboat Books:

Kazim Ali
Elizabeth Motika
Benjamin Taylor

This book has been made possible, in part, by a grant from the New York State Council on the Arts Literature Program.

State of the Arts

NYSCA